Praise for More Mo

Bill Witt was a godsend for our family. We met him in 2004 during a very stressful time when my father became Ill and had to go into a nursing home. He took the time to educate us on several options that would financially benefit my parents for their future. Tara, his partner, was also extremely helpful when my mother's health started to decline. She was able to help us apply for VA Benefits for home health care so my mother could stay in her house as long as possible.

Since that time Bill and Tara have guided us, family members and friends that needed assistance in planning their financial future. They have led us to a stream of steady income after retirement so we can have a comfortable life style with few worries.

Bill and Tara are professional, informative and always there to answer questions. They go above and beyond to ensure you and your family are protecting assets and income from future economic downturns. They are soft spoken and explain situations in laymen's terms with gentle guidance. They take their fiduciary responsibilities seriously. They are like family.

—Carol & Rocky S. of Round Rock, TX

My business partner and I sold our business of 24 years in 2012, and my wife and I decided to retire at that time. We were in search of a financial advisor and a smart place to invest our savings. We had heard positive things about Bill Witt and Senior Resource Center through my wife's employer. After also making inquiries elsewhere, we felt this was the place for us. Each year since has proved we were right. We get complete information, explanations and processes. Bill is an excellent advisor who speaks plainly, as if he were guiding a family member.

—William and Judy P. of Round Rock, TX

I am a veteran of the U.S. Air Force. At age 87, my wife and I had to sell our home and move into an Independent Living facility because of my health. Because of additional necessary "home care" expenses, we needed financial help. We learned about Bill Witt and his partner, Tara Kendrick, of Senior Resource Center. We called them and I'm glad we did. We could not have been more pleased with their professionalism and their friendliness. It was so easy working with them. They carefully guided us through the process with all the forms the VA requested from us. They were very knowledgeable about the process. They helped us submit our request on August 27, 2019, and we received notice of our approval on April 16, 2020. We couldn't be more appreciative of their help process. We highly recommend them to anyone who is seeking VA benefits.

—Don and Jane C. of Austin, TX

It is with my utmost respect and trust that I recommend Bill Witt and Tara Kendrick from Senior Resource Center. Four years ago, we needed help to get Medicaid for our mother with Alzheimer's. Faced with placing her in a nursing home for specialized care, this was a very stressful time. Thankfully, my friend recommended Senior Resource Center. Immediately, we knew we were in the right place! Bill Witt met with us for an extended amount of time and explained how he could help us get what we needed. To top it off, he charged a very reasonable price (a fraction compared to other companies). He and his partner, Tara Kendrick, walked us through the entire process. Set up an appointment for a free consultation. You won't regret it!

—Lori M. of Leander, TX

MORE MONEY
FOR RETIREMENT
YOUR GUIDE TO A BULLETPROOF FUTURE

WILLIAM C. WITT

2nd Half Coach and Retirement Specialist

Dedication

To Shasta Neely, the dear, sweet lady that helped launch my financial planning career. I started my career offering Medicaid counseling. I like to think of it as performing financial brain surgery, without medical school, but with the help of my trusty nurse Shasta. Shasta was my kind and caring mentor for two years. I thank God for Shasta Neely.

To the families we've helped with retirement planning, we thank you for trusting us to guide you in some of the biggest decisions you'll make in your lives. As a referral-based practice, we only grow when clients refer other families for our help. So, we especially want to thank all the families we've helped, that have referred others to us.

To our expert affiliates that help us offer comprehensive retirement, tax, long term care and estate planning, we appreciate you. You've helped polish the retirement plans for our clients, offering them the wide-ranging plans they deserve. Thank you, our trusted partners.

Finally, and most importantly, to my business partner, Tara Kendrick. Many great ideas come from great partnerships. In 2009 my phone rang and the voice on the other end said, "I want to do what you do." From that our partnership was born. Tara, you've made the last 10+ years fun. In many ways you've helped me write this book because the ideas that are included are the result of research, planning and positive outcomes we've seen for our clients as we worked side by side. Thank you, Tara!

Table of Contents

List of Figures

Introduction

Thank you, Coronavirus! I realize that sounds like a crazy way to start a book, but throughout life I've learned that good things sometimes come as a result of difficult times. And this is certainly no exception. Quarantined in my home in Burnet, TX for two months led me to an "ah-ha" moment. I saw our business in a new light, where the underlying theme was how we help people create more money for retirement. I call this addition of money, **extra money**.

Senior Resource Center (SRC) offers comprehensive retirement, tax, long-term care and estate planning. Why is it important to address all four areas? Like a puzzle that only shares a complete picture when you have all of the pieces arranged properly, we've found that **in order to build bulletproof retirement plans, you have to understand and integrate many disciplines, including Social Security, Medicare, Medicaid, VA, an array of financial products, the tax code, some legal stuff, with a little philosophy sprinkled in.** Said another way, having a financial advisor or stockbroker, isn't the same as having a comprehensive retirement plan. If I help you grow your retirement savings, but fail to protect your savings from catastrophic medical or long-term care expenses or taxes, how effective would the plan be? Probably like Swiss cheese - with more than a few holes.

At SRC we use powerful software that can forecast your financial situation to 10, 20 or even 30 years in the future. The models we build demonstrate how **extra money** creates safer, more enjoyable retirement lifestyles. It makes a BIG difference in how much our clients can spend on lifestyle and still leave a legacy for their children. **Extra money** is real money.

So, what is **extra money**? It's money anyone can create before and during retirement, **with just a little bit of planning**. It's a series of opportunities that many people overlook because they don't know they exist. If knowledge is power, think of this book as the roadmap to **extra money**.

So, where do you find **extra money**? Lots of places. If I can show you how to pay less income tax, that's **extra money**. If you can avoid medical and long-term care expenses, that's more **extra money**. And if you understand how Social Security, Medicare, Medicaid and VA benefits work, you'll find even more **extra money**.

There are two underlying themes in this narrative: **Control the things you can Control**, and **Income is more important than Assets**. Many of the factors we encounter in retirement are outside our control: stock market gyrations; Federal Reserve policies setting interest rates; future tax rates; political upheavals; and pandemics, to name a few. The **extra money** strategies in this book are based on things you CAN control. The second theme, the **Power of Income** in retirement planning is only now being recognized within the financial industry. Look at the financial industry ads appearing on television today. The "Income" word has suddenly become a lot more popular. While most financial advisors focus on asset growth, Tara and I have taken a financial road a lot less traveled. Over the years we've found that families with more guaranteed income in retirement have better financial outcomes. And the models we build continue to confirm the power of income.

This book describes many of the **extra money** strategies Tara and I have developed, helping thousands of families. It's our way of giving back some of the knowledge we've acquired. If you add just of few of the ideas in this book to your retirement planning, we assure you that your life will be at least a little bit better.

Finally, a word of caution. This book contains controversial financial concepts. Some may seem counterintuitive, and some will fly in the face of everything you and I have been taught since 3rd grade.

Near the end of the movie, *Pearl Harbor* (starring Ben Affleck and Alec Baldwin), Colonel Doolittle addresses a group of young American pilots. He tells them about a top-secret mission he's planning. It's very dangerous. Doolittle is planning the unthinkable: somehow launch American bombers from the short flight deck of one of our carriers, and bomb mainland Japan. He asks the men, "Everyone brave enough, step forward." Of course, they all do. Here is my challenge to you. If you are open to a different way of looking at retirement planning, willing to consider the unthinkable, step forward (keep reading). Like me, you just might see retirement planning in a whole new light.

Our Secret Sauce

In the beginning (the summer of 2002) I was descending Mount Olympus. No, not the famous mountain in Greece where Thor and Zeus live. I'm talking about a financial Mount Olympus. I was preparing for a long and comfortable early retirement when something unfortunate occurred. My millions – dot com paper millions that is – had suddenly dematerialized. Transitioning from dot com millionaire to average Joe, motivated me to seek a new career. My good friend Jerry, who lives in the valley (south Texas for non-Lone Star folks) told me his son was doing financial workshops in Austin, TX. He suggested sitting in on a workshop to explore a new career. I asked him what experience or credentials I would need, and he said "just an insurance license." I remember my exact thoughts at that moment: "There is no way in Hell I will ever be a low life insurance agent." Boy, have I learned to eat those words.

Tara and I build bulletproof retirement plans. What's our secret sauce? **We use very specific insurance products, in unique ways, to build bulletproof solutions for our clients.** Please read the last sentence 3 times. Over the years, many people have told me, "I hate insurance products." In the summer of 2002, I would have agreed. If you've heard all the bad news about insurance products, you have to make a decision right now. Either everything in this book is poppy cock or maybe, just maybe, some of what you've been told about insurance is poppy cock.

Do you want your savings to outperform the stock market? Would you like to get extra money from your IRA? Do you want to pay less income tax? Do you want to eliminate medical expenses and get someone else to pay for your long-term care? Would you like to have lots of tax free extra money and income in retirement? If you answered yes to any of these questions, I will show you how. Sometimes the financial road rarely traveled can offer some amazing opportunities. As I said in the introduction, if you're brave enough, step forward and turn the page.

Longevity…Blessing and Curse

Author's note: this chapter doesn't contain any **extra money** strategies and it doesn't mention insurance. What it does explain is why having more **extra money** in retirement is vital. Simple answer? We're living a lot longer, which means our retirement savings must last a lot longer <u>and</u> avoid a gauntlet of risks.

The next time you have five minutes free, try Googling "What was the average life expectancy in the Stone Age?" Then ask about Roman times, medieval times and 1900. Any guesses? The number doesn't change much, it's always somewhere near 30 years. Finally, ask what the average life expectancy in the United States is in 2020. The answer: 78.93 years. So, what happened around 1900? We obviously got a lot smarter medically. Today, doctors fix most medical issues and keep us in the game. We also have much better hygiene, and we understand how different foods, smoking and other factors affect our bodies. The good news…most of us will get to enjoy a much longer life. So, what's the bad news? Our money must last a lot longer to support our lifestyle. Why is this an issue? Living longer in retirement means exposing our savings to a litany of risks. Think about stock-market corrections, inflation, overspending, taxes, medical bills, long-term care expenses, creditors, lawsuits, identity theft, scams and incapacity to name just a few. Longevity means running a financial marathon where one misstep can lead to disaster.

The concept of "retirement" is a 20th century phenomenon. Most people in earlier time periods worked until they died. The notion of working 40+ years and retiring well for another 30 years would have seemed preposterous. If I published this book in 1900, there wouldn't be many takers, because virtually no one retired.

If you plan on being in retirement comfortably for 20+ years, this book is for you.

One-Minute Budget

People tell me creating a budget is tedious. Since I agree, I'm going to show you two ways to create a retirement budget in about one minute. You may be thinking, this book is supposed to be about **extra money**, why do we need a budget? You can't build a bullet-proof retirement plan unless you have a financial target in mind: the amount of money you need monthly while in retirement in order to enjoy life. I call this your **happy number**. We need to create enough **extra money** so that you can comfortably spend your **happy number** each month without going broke. And over time, we need to increase your **happy number** to keep up with inflation.

There are two very simple ways to find your **happy number:** checking and credit card statements or answering 7 questions.

If you pay your bills using a checking account (including debit cards) and credit cards, gather up 3 months of statements. I wouldn't use statements from the first half of 2020 because being quarantined means we probably spent less. Add up what you spent over a three-month period, divide it by 3, and that's a pretty good indicator of your average monthly **happy number**.

The second method is even simpler. Take out a piece of paper and write down 7 numbers. Don't overthink this, write down the number that comes to mind. What do you spend on **housing** (mortgage, rent, utilities, property insurance, phone, cable, internet), **living expense** (food, dining out, clothing and personal care), **healthcare and insurance** (health, life and long-term care), **transportation** (auto loans, insurance, fuel and repairs), **entertainment** (travel and parties), **education and loans** (tuition, credit cards, alimony and child support) and **miscellaneous** (donations, gifts, other). Add these guestimates and you're probably pretty close to your **happy number**.

If you are close to paying off your mortgage, car payments, student loans or supporting a child, adjust your **happy number** by what you won't be spending and don't forget to back out retirement contributions you will no longer need to save. If you're still working, don't adjust monthly expenses because you assume you will spend less when retired. Extra time has a way of creating new and exciting spending opportunities.

Our job in the rest of this book is to find **extra money** to support your **happy number**.

The Power of Income

Author's second note: this chapter doesn't contain any **extra money** strategies either. But don't fret, the rest of this book is ALL about **extra money**. What it does explain is why retirement models based on guaranteed lifetime income outperform models based on asset growth. The simple answer? You can create guaranteed lifetime income (ideally tax-free lifetime income that increases) but you can't guarantee stock market performance.

Sometime around 2010 I read a financial column in the newspaper that got me thinking. The column began with an interesting question: What is the most important factor that protects people from going broke in retirement? When I read the answer, I said "well duh" that's obvious. The primary factor: people with more guaranteed income don't go broke in retirement. Think about it. If you have money coming in each month, just like when you're working, even if your savings go to $0, you still have income and you still have money to spend.

When Tara and I started building retirement models for clients, the power of lifetime income (especially if it's tax free) consistently provided better outcomes. And then a second light bulb went off. Income is something you and I can create, something we can control. Today, there are great products that create lifetime income. Some of them increase the income over time, some eventually become tax free and some double if your health fails and you need long-term care.

Still not sold on the power of income? If you are an Arby's fan, you're thinking "Bill, show me the meat." In 2019 The Principal Financial Group commissioned a study conducted by Michael Finke, Ph.D., CFP, and Wade Pfau, Ph.D., CFP, nationally renowned researchers from The American College (who are not affiliated with Principal). They ran 10,000 Monte Carlo simulations (in layman's terms, a lot of number crunching) to see how income impacts retirement savings. Here are their words: *"The research revealed how retirees can use guaranteed income annuities to not only* **improve financial outcomes,** *but also* **increase confidence and reduce stress in retirement.**... *Retirees who have purchased an annuity are more confident than those without one... They worry less about the market, feel more comfortable spending on things they enjoy and feel they have a better life with less worry of outliving their savings.*[1]" **Improved financial outcomes, increased confidence and reduced stress in retirement.** I couldn't have said it better myself. Actually, Tara and I have been saying it for the past 10 years. The Finke/Pfau study is interesting. Half of their report focuses on better financial outcomes, which might be expected. But interestingly, half of the report explains the impact of income on human emotion, the positive impact income has on people's confidence that their money will last, that they can confidently spend in retirement, and be able to leave a legacy to their children. Do you want more **Peace of Mind** in retirement? I can help you find it. Click: https://401kspecialistmag.com/study-by-finke-pfau-shows-annuities-improve-retirement-outcomes/ or email me at bill@srctexas.com for a copy of the Finke/Pfau report.

Finally, why do I favor income-based retirement planning versus asset growth-based planning? As long as the market is up 5 or 6% every year, asset growth-based plans work just fine. Throw in a market correction and you have to start thinking Biblically, where there's "weeping and gnashing of teeth." I'm not into gnashing. You and I can't control the stock market. We can hope the market goes up, but building a retirement plan based on hope is a slippery slope. For the record, I am NOT opposed to asset growth. To prove my point, in the next chapter I'm going to show you how to safely grow your savings. In fact, let me make a bold prediction. I'm going to show you how to outperform the stock market with NO risk. Not possible? Read the next chapter.

Beat the Market

Author's third note: This chapter includes a discussion of stock market investments. Since Tara and I are not securities licensed, please refer ALL risk-investment questions to a licensed securities professional. This chapter is merely my opinion as a fellow citizen.

The United States suffers from a national addiction. I'm not talking about Opioids. I'm talking about gambling! No, not the hordes of people that descend on Las Vegas for a game of chance. I'm talking about investing in the stock market. I think of it as legalized gambling. For as long as I can remember, the financial industry has suggested that the easy way to wealth is riding the stock market roller coaster. Every night the evening news reports the daily movement of the Dow Jones, S&P 500 and Nasdaq indexes. After a few years of happy growth, we get seduced into thinking "everybody else is making money, why not me?" If you love the stock market roller coaster, this chapter is for YOU.

True confession… I hate losing money, but I want my money to grow. So, years ago I started looking for a safer way to grow my money and my client's money. I call my investment strategy Tortoise Investing. Remember the Tortoise and Hare race? If you are invested in the stock market today, you are probably a Hare investor. Tortoise Investing is different. It's based on two simple principals: eliminate fees and avoid market corrections. Do these two things, and you too can beat the market.

First, let me define what I mean by the market. What benchmark do I compare my performance against? Everyone has heard of the Dow Jones and S&P 500 indexes. The Dow index consists of 30 large companies, while the S&P includes 500 large companies. Many economists think the S&P 500 is a better (broader) economic barometer of the U.S. economy. If the S&P is rising, our economy is growing. I measure my performance against the S&P 500.

But there's another factor we have to include to use the S&P as our benchmark. You can't invest in the market without incurring fees. Some of the fees are visible and some are hidden. If you have a financial advisor, you are probably paying that person a fee to manage your money. It's often a percentage of your money under management. This is the visible fee that shows up in your statements. If you Google "What does a stockbroker typically charge to manage money" you get a range of fees, typically between 1 and 2%. Let's be conservative and use 1% as the visible fee we pay each year. The second fee many people pay is based on the investments they've selected. Many people like mutual funds. Mutual funds are groups of stocks and bonds that have a similar characteristic. The characteristic might be based on a specific industry, geographic area or size of company. The people that create mutual funds charge a fee to manage them. Their fees are usually hidden. They are deducted from the fund's performance but are not broken out where you see what you're paying. I have access to a website that pinpoints the fees charged by each mutual fund. If you want to know what you're really paying, come see me. Mutual fund fees range from less than .1% to over 2%. Let's use 1% as our hidden fee. Adding the two fees together: 1% visible and 1% hidden, I often find people are paying 2% per year. That's not a lot, but if you are with your broker 10 years how much have you paid in fees? 2% x 10 = 20% of your money. Eliminate the fees and you just found some **extra money**.

The second principal of Tortoise Investing is avoiding market corrections. As I write this book, the Coronavirus is hammering our economy. From almost no unemployment, we've risen to 13% unemployment in 6 short weeks. The stock market has also corrected, from Dow highs near 30,000 to 25,000. Market corrections occur every few years. In 2000, we had the dot com meltdown and in 2008, it was the great recession caused by mortgage-backed securities. Bull (up) and Bear (down) markets are part of history. But what if there was a way to avoid the Bear? What if your savings rose in the Bull market cycles but didn't drop when the market corrected? This is where I've found more **extra money**.

Here's the Tortoise investing proposition I offer my clients. In a good year (assuming the stock market is up) you can earn up to 5%. If the market is up 2%, you get 2%. If the market is up 10%, you only get 5%. But what happens when the market drops? You get a zero that year, no growth, but no loss.

So how has Tortoise Investing done since 2000? Figure 1 shows how a $100,000 investment performed invested in the S&P 500 Index. Note: I assumed a 1% annual management fee. Your actual fee might be higher or lower. Figure 1 also shows Tortoise performance. From 2000 to 2002 when the market dropped, my clients didn't make any money, but they didn't lose any money. When the market started growing (2003 – 2007) my clients participated, but remember, upside is always capped at 5%. Figure 1 summarizes performance from 2000 to 2020. Which line do you want to be on? I like being high water, where part of my money isn't missing. The chart may look like a dead heat, but remember, what happened in early 2020… COVID-19. I declare Tortoise the winner.

But this isn't the whole story. What didn't we do from 2000 to 2020? Withdraw any funds! What if I retired in 2000 and had to start tapping my savings for living expenses? What if this was an IRA and I was forced to take Required Minimum Distributions? (More on this in the chapter: Extra Money from Retirement Accounts). The timing of withdrawals affects your money.

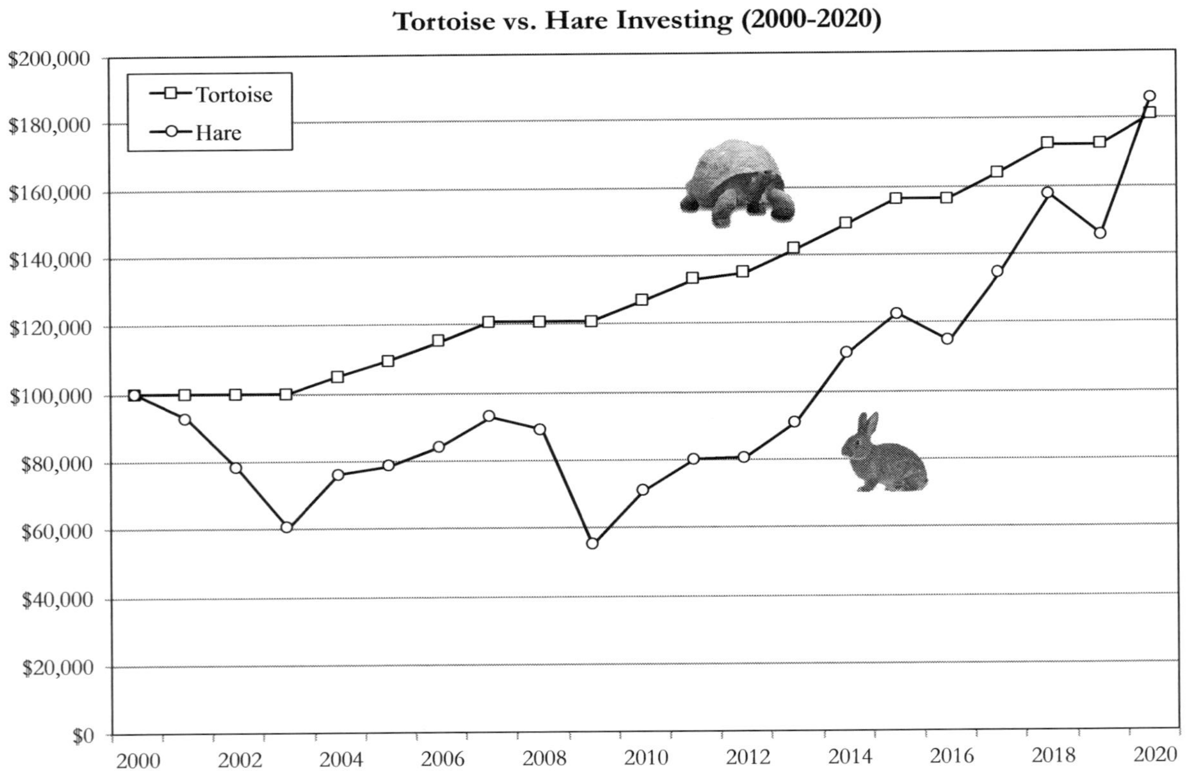
Tortoise vs. Hare Investing (2000-2020)
Tortoise
Hare
$200,000
$180,000
$160,000
$140,000
$120,000
$100,000
$80,000
$60,000
$40,000
$20,000
$0
2000
2002
2004
2006
2008
2010
2012
2014
2016
2018
2020

Figure 1

To prove my point, let's assume you withdraw $5,000 annually. Figure 2 tells the story. Unfortunately, the Hare doesn't make it to the finish line. **The timing of withdrawals and market corrections has a major impact on your financial outcome.**

Ok, I know what your next question is. What is the magic product that grows when the market rises, avoids market corrections and has no management fees? They've been around for years, but I'll bet your broker has never mentioned them. They are tax-deferred annuities offered by insurance companies. So, if they're so great, why hasn't your broker mentioned them? Simple answer. How does your broker make money? He (she) gets an annual fee to manage your money. Put money in an annuity and your advisor gets a one-time commission, i.e., no multi-year pay day. That's a little harsh, but money talks.

Does anyone else think annuities may be a good option to safely grow your retirement funds? Some very bright guys in the financial industry (well above my pay grade) have done research and written papers. Robert Shiller, PhD at Yale University, creator of the Shiller Barclays CAPE Index family and recently recognized as one of the top 50 financial minds in the world, and Roger Ibbotson, PhD, Chairman of Zebra Capital Management and Professor Emeritus of Finance at Yale School of Management, to name a few. Here's what a paper Robert Shiller co-authored said. *"Fixed Index Annuity (FIA) returns were impressive in a historical simulation… an FIA structure, if well designed offers a potentially beneficial alternative investment for a retirement portfolio… By combining a principal guarantee with a degree of stock market participation FIAs appear to offer a risk/reward profile that differs from either bonds or stocks alone.*[2]*"* That's high level financial speak for they may be a good idea. Roger Ibbotson is more to the point. *"FIAs have many attractive features as both an accumulation investment and as a potential source of income in retirement.*[3]*"* Tortoise agrees! I'd be happy to send you their white papers.

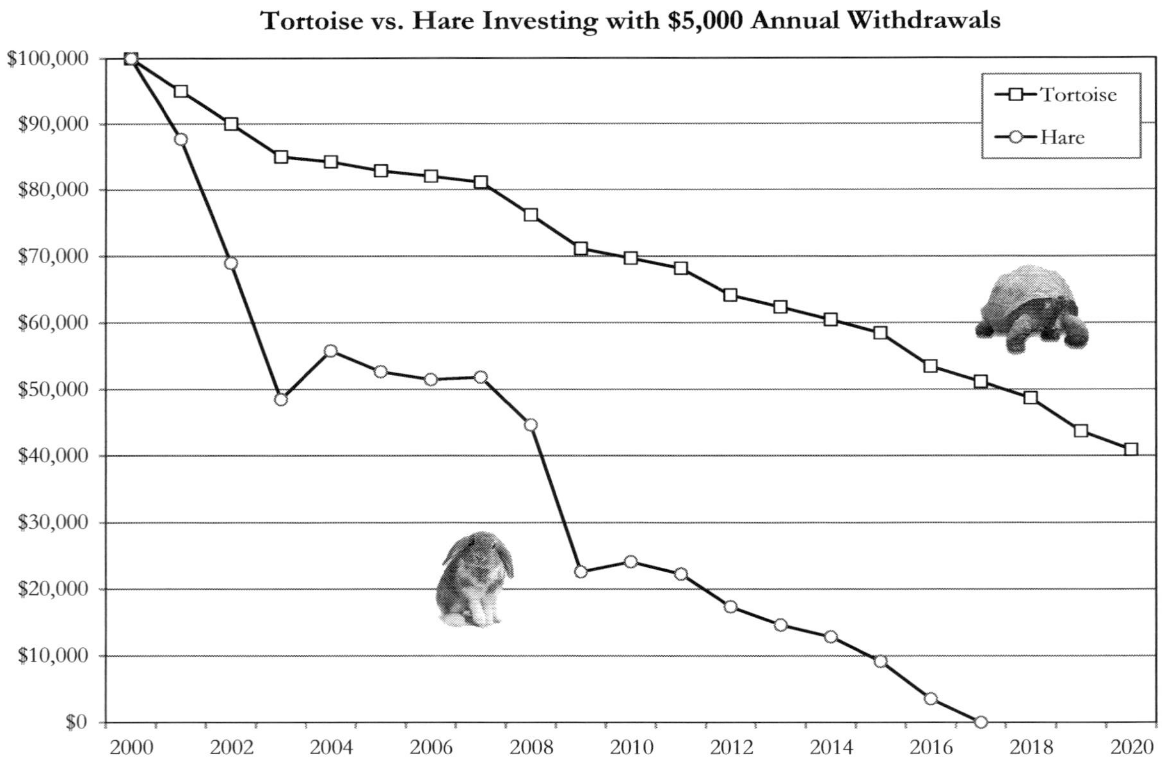

Tortoise vs. Hare Investing with $5,000 Annual Withdrawals

Figure 2

One final point on the stock market: I'm NOT against investing in the market. I believe in diversified investments when planning for retirement, and market investments have their place. But, pinning your financial future and peace of mind on a "market only" strategy that you can't control is risky. If you build a solid foundation first using annuities to ensure your lifestyle, based on safe growth and guaranteed income, you'll then have the freedom to comfortably explore market opportunities with the rest of your money.

Tara and I help clients safely grow retirement assets using tax-deferred annuities. Like any product type, some annuities perform better than others. We help clients find best-in-class annuities. Numbers don't lie. For the past 20 years, we've beaten the market, creating **extra money** for our clients. Since the beginning of COVID-19, I've had a lot of very happy client phone calls. If you'd like to explore the features and benefits of deferred annuities, give us a call.

The "I" Word

You probably think I'm going to talk about Insurance. Nope. This chapter focuses on another risk we face in retirement: Inflation. I want to explain how Inflation affects us and why another "trusted" form of investing, Bonds, may not be a good idea.

So, what is inflation? Everything gets more expensive over time. Think about what you paid for your first car. How does that compare to the one you own today? My first car was a 1967 VW Beetle. It had a base sticker price of $1,639. Today I drive a 2014 Toyota Prius that cost me $22,000. Both are economy cars, but that's a 1,342% increase in price. That's the impact of inflation.

If a dozen eggs cost $1.00 today and we have 3% annual inflation, what would eggs cost in 25 years? The answer: $2.03. If we want to enjoy retirement for an extended period of time, our spendable income, our **happy number**, must keep up with rising costs.

So, what causes inflation? Economists talk about two factors: rising government debt and printing more money. Here's where this story gets a little scary. Both factors have been rising. U.S. government debt as a percentage of our Gross Domestic Product (GDP)[4] has been rising since the early 1980's. Figure 3 tells the story. In 2020, with massive spending to offset the economic impact of the Coronavirus, financial experts forecast the U.S. will exceed the high-water mark of 120%[5] (government debt as a % of GDP) set at the end of World War II. With spending on future entitlement programs (Social Security, Medicare and Medicaid) expected to rise, this percentage may continue to go up. To make matters worse, what did the Federal Reserve start doing in 2008 to revive the U.S. economy after the great recession? Buy lots of government and private debt. The Federal Reserve's balance sheet (refer to Figure 4) has ballooned from $870 Billion in

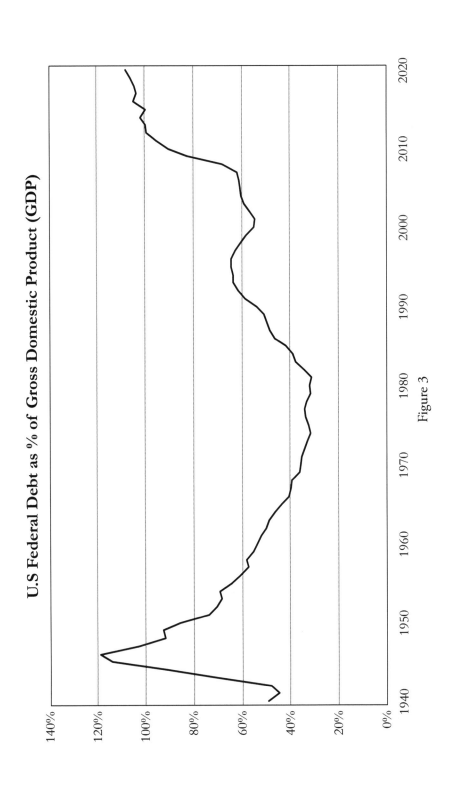

U.S Federal Debt as % of Gross Domestic Product (GDP)

Figure 3

August 2007 to over \$7 Trillion in June 2020[6]. When the Federal Reserve buys debt, it prints money, lots of money, to acquire the debt. With government deficits and money printing skyrocketing, do you think we just might see some inflation?

Tara and I have two ways to help you plan ahead for the higher costs caused by inflation. Some of the annuities we offer have income payouts, that once activated, continue to increase if the stock market is up. That's a great way to keep up with inflation. Other annuities that emphasize growth or help pay for future long-term care, have level payouts that don't increase over time. You can use multiple annuities with level payments as a defense against inflation. Our clients activate income streams, one at a time, when more income is needed. If our clients never activate the income, the full account value that has grown safely passes to their children. If they've activated income and there's still value in the annuity when they die, that money also passes to their children.

Finally, a word of caution (remember, I do NOT have a securities license, this is just my opinion). Bonds are traditionally considered a safer alternative to stocks. Bonds pay a defined interest rate and they have performed very well over the last 40 years. Why? The value of a bond fluctuates inversely to rising and falling interest rates. When interest rates rise, the underlying value of a bond drops, and conversely, when interest rates drop, the value of a bond rises. If I own a bond that pays 4% and interest rates drop, my higher earning bond is now more valuable. Since 1980 bond interest rates have been declining, which means bond investors have done well. But, with interest rates near zero today, which way do you think interest rates will go in the future? They can't get much lower. Then think about how the Federal Reserve fights excessive inflation. They raise interest rates. Growing government deficits and printing more money could lead to inflation

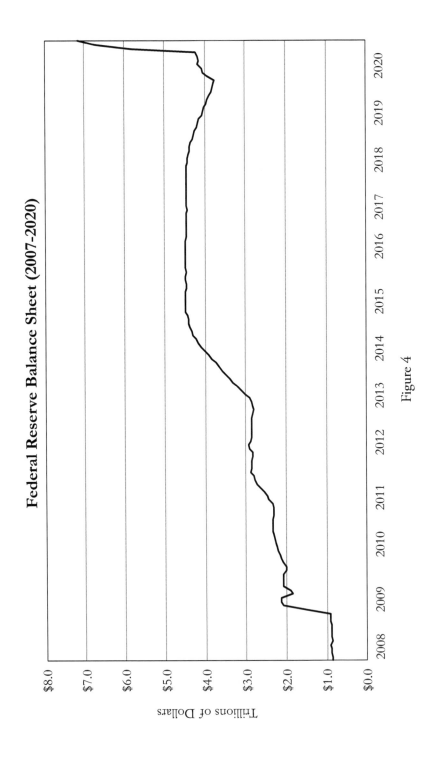

Figure 4

and the Federal Reserve raising interest rates to control it. What will happen to bond values if all this unfolds? The white paper co-authored by Robert Shiller mentioned earlier in the Beat the Market chapter, discusses how Fixed Index annuities may be a better, safer alternative than bonds.

Maximize Your Social Security

Social Security is an important building block in creating your **happy number** and it's a great source of **extra money.** Draw benefits for several years and you'll see we all get some **extra money**. It's also one of the few sources of income in retirement that increase with the cost of living. Since everything gets more expensive over time, having income that keeps up with inflation is very nice.

While we work and contribute to Social Security, we create a future lifetime pension. We can claim income benefits as early as 62 or as late as 70. The longer we delay benefits, the more we get. But here's an interesting secret regarding Social Security: When President Roosevelt introduced Social Security in the 1930's, the original actuarial payout assumed people would only live into their mid 60's, i.e., only receive a few years of benefits. The reality is, we're living a lot longer. If you analyze how much you and your employer pay in during your working years, after about 10 years (could be longer or shorter based on your income) most of us have received ALL of the deposits back, and presto, now we're getting **extra money**. That's the easy part. Assuming we live long enough drawing Social Security, we all get **extra money**. But the real trick is maximizing what we get from Social Security over our lifetime, getting more **extra money**. Tara and I help people make smart claiming decisions, pinpointing when to claim and which Social Security benefit to claim to maximize their lifetime payout. We often increase the lifetime payout for a couple by more than $200,000, and sometimes more than $300,000. Now that's a lot of **extra money!**

When Should You Claim?
As a reminder, you can claim Social Security as early as 62 and as late as 70. So how will claiming age affect your benefit? Each of

us has a Full Retirement Age (FRA) between 66 and 67, depending on the year we were born. If we claim at our FRA, we get 100% of our retirement benefit based on how much we earned during our 35 top earning years. If we claim before our FRA we start with a reduced amount. How much is it reduced? If your FRA is 67 and you claim at 62, your starting benefit is reduced by 30%. Unfortunately, this is what many people do, and then often live to regret it. Yes, they get 5 additional years of benefits, but over time, cost of living adjustments will increase the difference in payouts.

Let's say you are 62, your age 67 benefit is projected to be $2,400 and the Cost of Living Adjustment (COLA) increase is 3% per year. If you claim at age 62, you start with a benefit of $1,680 (70% of $2,400). If you wait until age 67 the starting benefit has grown to $2,782 ($2,400 increased by 5 years of 3% COLA increases), or $834 more each month (remember, your age 62 benefit is increasing with COLA too). Over time COLA increases this gap and by the time you're 80 you're getting $1,225 more each month. That's a lot of **extra money**.

What if you wait until 70 to start claiming? Social Security benefits increase 8% each year that you delay benefits beyond your full retirement age. Your starting benefit at 70 would be $3,770 ($2,400 increased by 8 years of 3% COLA plus 3 years of 8% increases) or $1,641 more than your age 62 claimed benefit that has also increased with COLA. By age 80 the gap widens to $2,206 per month. That's a lot more **extra money**. Whether our 62 year old waits until 67 or 70, assuming he (she) lives into their late 70's, Figure 5 shows the lifetime payout is always greater. And if you're married and the family's primary breadwinner, and assuming your wife survives you (hint: ladies live longer), she steps up to your much higher survivor benefit. This is how couples increase lifetime payout by hundreds of thousands of dollars of **extra money**.

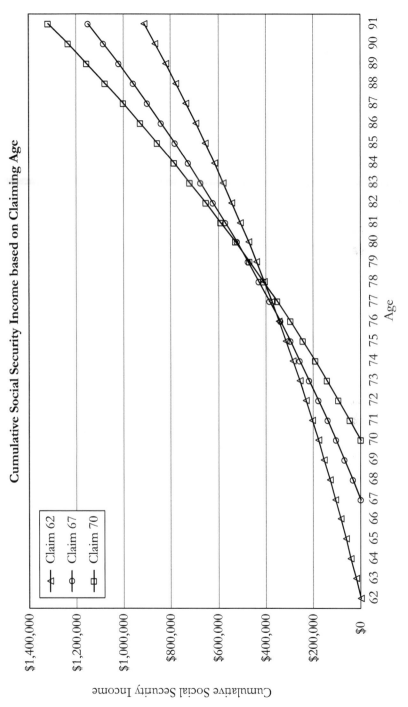

Figure 5

Which Benefit Should You Claim?

Here's the second factor that impacts your lifetime payout. Which benefit should you claim? If you're married, widowed or divorced (assuming the marriage lasted 10 years), you may have multiple benefits to choose from. You can always select a benefit based on your own work history, but sometimes claiming against your spouse's (or ex-spouse's) work history might pay more. And if you've been married more than once (each longer than 10 years) you may be able to select (or switch) between multiple survivor benefits.

If Social Security claiming seems more complex than you imagined, it is. Fortunately, we have a simple solution. Our calculator compares multiple claiming scenarios and shows you upfront how to maximize your lifetime payout, thus, how to get more **extra money**.

Extra Money from Retirement Accounts

Another source of **extra money** is not as obvious: tax-qualified retirement plans, including IRA, 401k, 403b and 457 plans. Federal Reserve data[7] from 2018 shows $9.2 Trillion in IRAs and another $6.5 Trillion in the other qualified plans. That's a lot of money. So, how do you get **extra money** out of your retirement accounts? First, you have to understand what the government forces you to do when you turn 72…start taking Required Minimum Distributions (RMDs). The tax penalty for not taking your RMD is significant. (Note: because of the Coronavirus, there are (were) no RMDs in 2020). The RMD % (i.e. the amount you must take each year) starts at about 4% at age 72 and increases as you get older.

RMD Dipping vs. Lifetime Income
So, what's the smartest way to take RMDs? Most people dip each year, withdrawing the appropriate amount. Over time as the RMD % increases, the value of the retirement account may go down, and so does the RMD amount. But what if there was a better way to satisfy the RMD requirement, where the annual payment you received would actually **increase**? Tara and I show clients how to add a lifetime pension to their retirement accounts. The pension amount satisfies the RMD requirement and increases (never declines) based on growth in the stock market. So, where's the **extra money**? Our models show that adding the lifetime pension pays out all your IRA (including growth) around age 85, when it goes to $0. But remember the pension is lifetime, and if you're married, it continues to pay out no matter which spouse is alive. So, do you think you or your spouse might live beyond 85? If so, the checks will keep coming. Hence, more **extra money**.

Make it Tax Free

But wait, there's another opportunity for even more **extra money**! What do you have to do when you take an RMD or lifetime pension payment? **Pay taxes!** Now here's where we get creative. When your retirement account is almost depleted, we convert the taxable IRA to a tax-free Roth IRA and voila, the remaining life-time payments are: **TAX FREE.** This is like giving you or your spouse a raise in your mid 80's.

What product creates this lifetime pension? It's the same product I described earlier that safely outperforms the stock mar-ket – a tax-deferred annuity with an additional income rider fea-ture. Rolling over your IRA to a tax-deferred annuity is a simple, tax-free exchange. Live long, you get extra tax money. Live short, your kids inherit your IRA. Getting **extra money** from your IRA takes a little planning. Call us and we'll show you how to do it.

Eliminate Medical Bills

Medical care has gotten really expensive! In December 2019, I got a call from Jerry Grote. Jerry is one of my famous clients. He was the catcher on the 1969 New York Mets team, the Miracle Mets that won the World Series. He called and said, "Thank you." Since we hadn't talked in several years, I asked "What are you thanking me for?" He told me several years earlier he wasn't feeling good and went into a hospital to have some medical tests. While there he had a heart attack, triple bi-pass surgery and spent eleven days in intensive care. When he got home and got the bill, it was over $1,000,000. He went on to say the Medicare coverage I helped him get was great. He paid $0. Wow! Talk about **extra money**. Spend a few days or weeks in a hospital with the wrong Medicare insurance and you'd better be related to Bill Gates or Michael Dell if you want to avoid bankruptcy.

Medicare is one of the few reasons it will feel good to get older in this country. When we turn 65 most of us will qualify for Medicare benefits from the government, based on our work history or our spouse's work history. Make the right choices and you can create coverage with NO co-pays and little or NO deductibles at the doctor, lab or hospital. Equally important, you can go to almost all the doctors, specialists, hospitals, labs and clinics. You pick the providers!

So how does this work and what are your options? Tara and I like to make complex issues simple. As an example, Figure 6 shows all your Medicare options on a single sheet of paper. Compare this to the *Medicare and You* book from the U.S. government each year or the flood of printed and electronic advertising you get each year in the fall. By simply understanding our single page Medicare Options chart, you're ready to make some choices.

2020 Medicare Health Care Options

Original Medicare

Advantage Medicare

Part D – Prescription Drug Coverage
Annual Plan (Jan 1 to Dec 31)
CoPays / Doughnut Hole

Use www.medicare.gov to Identify Plan
with Lowest Annual Cost

Medicare Supplement / Medigap
Lifetime Plan
11 Standard Plans (A – N)

Plan F – No CoPays or Deductibles
* Monthly Premium

Part A
Hospital / Nursing Home

No Premium

$1,408 Deductible/Benefit
Period
Co-Pay based on # of days

Part B
Doctor / Laboratory

** $144.60 / Month

$198 Annual Deductible
Co-Pay 80% / 20%
(Excess Charge 15%)

Part C – Advantage Plans
Annual Plan (Jan 1 to Dec 31)

PPO – Open Network (In or Out)
HMO – Closed Network (In Only)
PFFS – No Network
SNP – Special Needs Plan

Use www.medicare.gov to Identify Plan
with Lowest Annual Cost

No Underwriting (Medical Questions)
No Deductibles
CoPays for Everything
Plans may include Drug Coverage
*** Monthly Premium

* Monthly Premium varies by plan, age, zip code and tobacco usage
** Monthly Premium varies by income   *** Monthly Premium varies by plan

Senior Resource Center • 4408 Spicewood Springs Road • Austin, TX 78759 • Office 512-835-0963

Figure 6

You'll see that our chart shows two Medicare options: Original Medicare and Medicare Advantage. Original Medicare has been around since the late 1960's. You'll sign up for Medicare Part A (your hospital and rehabilitation coverage) and Medicare Part B (doctor and lab coverage) through the Social Security administration. Part A is free, and Part B has a monthly premium based on your income (as of 2020, most people pay $144.60 per month). Parts A and B have deductibles and co-pays (places where you must pay out of pocket). Private insurance companies now offer eleven types of Medicare Supplements (insurance products also known as Medigap policies - Plans A through N) to cover some of or all the deductibles and co-pays. That's how Medicare looked until 2006 when the government rolled out Part D prescription drug plans to help defray the cost of drugs. I will save a discussion on prescription drug plans for the next chapter because these plans bring their own issues and opportunities.

The second Medicare option, Advantage Plans, also debuted in 2006. Advantage plans often include drug coverage. Think of Advantage plans as a fully privatized version of Medicare offered by an insurance company. You still pay your Medicare B premium, but all your claims are processed by the insurance company, not the government.

So which option is better for you? Let's find out.

Supplements vs. Advantage Plans

We've been selling Supplements for a long time. In 2006, we also began offering Advantage plans. In the past we would explain the pros and cons of both options and talk through the options to help our clients get the coverage they want. Today, based on a lot of feedback from clients, we are more specific and guided in our recommendations and normally try to steer our clients away from Advantage Plans.

Why is this and how do the options compare? Medicare supplements have been around since the late 1960's. Almost all medical providers accept them, i.e., you have freedom of choice. Premiums vary depending on the supplement company and plan you pick. Let's say the starting monthly premium is $130 per month. With a supplement you should expect the premium to increase annually as you get older. Supplements eliminate most or all deductibles and co-pays at the doctor, lab and hospital. You essentially know your financial exposure to medical events. It's the monthly premium you pay.

What about Advantage plans? Advantage plans offer much lower monthly premiums; they usually include drug coverage; they may include additional benefits such as vision and dental coverage not available with Medicare Supplements; and they are heavily marketed. So, what do we recommend? Tara and I have humorously renamed these plans disadvantage plans, and we no longer offer them. Why? Several reasons. The biggest factor is freedom to choose your medical provider. When you face a major medical event, you will likely want the ability to choose who will provide the care. Our experience is that Advantage plans have much smaller provider networks. Many of the Advantage plans offered today are HMO's, which means if you go out of network, you will pay the entire cost of treatment. Here's another quick story to drive this point home: Several years ago, I got a call from someone at M.D. Anderson in Houston. His wife had just completed chemotherapy, all paid for by their Advantage plan. In the morning's meeting with the Oncologist, they were told the next phase of her treatment would be Stem Cell therapy. Their Advantage plan covered Stem Cell therapy, but the plan did NOT have a contract with M.D. Anderson. In short, they had to find all new doctors. Adding salt to the wound, they were told that if they would have had original Medicare with a Supplement, it would have all been covered. As you can imagine, this gentleman was not happy. The second issue we have with Advantage plans are the hidden costs. Remember, with Supplements there can be minimal or no deductibles and co-pays. Advantage plans sometimes have unfortunate financial surprises. If you want to go with an Advantage plan, make sure to ask about all co-pays and deductibles, and make sure your doctors and care providers will accept that specific plan prior to signing up for it.

So where do Advantage plans fit in? If you are healthy and rubbing two nickels together to make ends meet, consider an Advantage plan. But if you can afford a higher monthly premium in your retirement budget, I'd recommend you go with a Supplement.

Save on Prescriptions

As mentioned earlier, Medicare prescription drug plans debuted in 2006 and are usually a standalone part of an Original Medicare solution or are included in a Medicare Advantage plan. Drug plans are only offered by private insurance companies. All stand-alone plans have monthly premiums (usually somewhere between $13 and $70 per month). Some plans have annual deductibles, typically $435 before they start to pay. And all plans have co-pays at the pharmacy based on the prescription's drug tier (preferred generic, non-preferred generic, preferred brand, non-preferred brand and specialty). Also, each plan has a formulary, or list of drugs that are covered. If a drug isn't in the formulary, it can be expensive. So, what is your best choice?

5 Minute Annual Checkup
With 24 standalone plans in Texas in 2020, how do you choose? The simple answer: find the plan with the lowest annual cost (what you're going to pay out of pocket over the next twelve months). Your annual cost includes your monthly premium, the deductible if there is one, and your co-pays. To help you, here's a great example of where the government got it right. We refer clients to www.medicare.gov to identify their most cost-effective option. In five minutes, you build a drug list by drug name, dosage and frequency and pick a pharmacy. This website ranks the plans by lowest annual cost. Think of it like going to the Kentucky Derby with 24 horses running, and this website pinpointing the winning horse for you.

So, where's the **extra money**? We've found that some people are lazy. They pick a plan, like their plan and get comfortable. But the plans change subtly each year, and these little changes can prove to be very expensive. We recommend re-visiting www.medicare.

gov annually between October 15th and December 7th to verify you will be on the most cost-effective plan for the coming year. Time for another story: A lady called mid-November saying she got our free newsletter recommending a trip to the Medicare website to check drug plans. She said that she liked her current drug plan. I told her I liked my drug plan too, but that I liked my wallet even more. I told her how to navigate the Medicare website. Getting to the last page she got confused and called back. She said, "Each plan has a different monthly premium and different co-pays; how do I choose?" I directed her to the "annual cost" column. I asked her what the annual cost of the winning plan was. She said "$1,600." I asked, "Is that the plan you like so much?" to which she replied "No." I asked her to scroll down and find the plan she liked. When she found it, the phone got very quiet. I asked how much her plan would cost for the coming year… $3,500! By switching, she saved $1,900. That's a lot of **extra money**.

One final suggestion regarding the Medicare website: The final page used to rank plans based on lowest annual cost. Now it default sorts based on lowest premium, which is usually not your best choice. Remember to re-sort the final page by 'lowest annual drug and premium cost' to find your most cost-effective option.

Medicare Insurance vs. GoodRx vs. Going North

Medicare drug coverage isn't always your most cost-effective solution. Several alternatives have arisen such as GoodRx. When I go to the pharmacy and find that my co-pay is expensive, I always ask, "what is the GoodRx price?" It never hurts to ask. Clients have shared another option that I can only mention. Some folks facing high co-pays have Googled pharmacies north of our border. With nationalized healthcare, Canada sometimes negotiates lower drug prices. I cannot recommend this as an option, I only mention it for educational purposes. Not sure if there's **extra money** north of the border.

Don't Pay for Long-Term Care

I say this because I have a very personal experience with this topic and have lived it firsthand. My dad was a successful businessman. When mom and pop retired, they had $1.2 million in savings, Social Security and pensions. Mom had a stroke at 82 and lived 14 years in a wheelchair, perky but paralyzed on her left side. A year after mom's stroke, pop was diagnosed with Alzheimer's disease and lived another 9 years. Much of their care was received in a facility. When mom went to heaven, my siblings and I divvied up $600,000. So, what's the moral of the story? Long-term care can be very expensive.

AARP agrees. Several years ago, they did a survey to find out why people go broke in retirement. Any guesses on the winner? Bernie Madoff? The Stock Market? Overspending? The winner (actually, the loser) was paying for long-term care. It's an uncomfortable topic to discuss, but when it happens, the financial impact can be devastating. How did this become the BIG ELEPHANT in the room? We're living a lot longer and sooner or later our brains or parts of our bodies wear out, requiring long-term care. To make matters worse, the cost of care (it's labor intensive) and the length of care keeps going up. Let's see if we can find some **extra money**.

Nursing Homes are Expensive
This section discusses Medicaid benefits. Since each state has its own unique eligibility rules, if you live in Texas, it's your lucky day and you can read on for specific details; if not, seek local expertise.

A nursing home is probably the last place most of us want to end up, and if we get there, the sticker shock can be very painful. As of 2020, the average monthly rate for a semi-private room in a nice nursing home in Austin, TX is around $6,000. And the cost of a private room is more like $7,500. That's a lot of money, month after month. So, let's find some **extra money** to help with that should you need it.

I bet you've heard that a person has to be destitute in order to qualify for Medicaid. Let me tell you that's absolute baloney! Tara and I have helped more than 1,300 families qualify for Medicaid benefits to help pay for nursing home care. Our goal is simple: preserve assets and qualify for benefits. And here's the good news: Most married couples in Texas can protect ALL of their assets (home, car and all their financial assets) and still qualify one spouse for Medicaid benefits. Single people can protect their home, car and usually 50 to 60% of their liquid assets and qualify for Medicaid benefits. The next time someone says, "You have to be broke," tell them to call us. The amount the nursing home resident must pay each month is a portion of their income, and with couples, sometimes that amount is as low as $0. Imagine a $6,000 nursing home bed for little or no dollars. That's a lot of **extra money**.

Getting **extra money** for long-term care takes some planning. Tara and I have different strategies to help protect your home, burial programs, retirement (IRA) funds and other assets. Your home is exempt (not counted) when you apply for Medicaid benefits, but after your death the State of Texas will try to recover from it what it spent on your care. If you re-deed your home using a Lady Bird Deed, there will be no estate recovery. We'll show you how to do this. What about protecting retirement accounts? The State of Texas exempts retirement accounts (IRAs 401ks, Roth IRAs, etc.) if the funds are held in one specific type of product. Any guesses as to which one? You got it. A tax-deferred annuity. IRA funds in a CD or brokerage account: COUNTABLE. IRA funds in a tax-deferred annuity: EXEMPT. Couples can protect all their other savings by setting up a spousal pension. This is another special type of annuity that protects funds that would normally be paid to the nursing home. Single people can protect 50 to 60% of their non-retirement funds by gifting funds to a son or daughter and then un-gifting, using some of the funds to pay for nursing home care. But what if your son or daughter gets divorced or sued and loses your gifted funds? No problem. We store the gifted funds in a tax-deferred annuity that is protected from creditors, lawsuits and divorce. They can't lose your money. Medicaid planning is one situation where getting professional guidance really pays off. Call us to discuss your situation.

Are you a Veteran?

Sometimes people need long-term care at home or in an Assisted Living facility, but don't need skilled nursing. Since Medicaid benefits are limited to skilled nursing, we ask a different question. Did you or your spouse serve active duty in the military during a war? Think WWII, Korea, Vietnam and the Gulf War. The VA has created a pension with Aid and Attendance for war-time veterans and their spouses when they need, are receiving and are paying for long-term care. The veteran does not have to have served in a combat zone or been injured in order to receive this benefit. Married veterans are eligible for more than $2,200 per month. Widows of war-time veterans are eligible for more than $1,200 per month. Both of these benefits are **extra money**. The rules to qualify for benefits are complicated and the application forms are a veritable minefield. As with Medicaid planning, help from an experienced guide is essential to getting the benefit. Call us. We can help.

The Insurance Option

Are there other ways to pay for long-term care beyond Medicaid and VA benefits? Yes, there are. There are four types of insurance products that provide **extra money** (getting someone else to pay for your care): traditional long-term care insurance, asset multiplying products, tapping the death benefit of a life insurance policy and doubling a pension payment. Each option has its pros and cons.

Long-term care insurance is a great way to pay for long-term care. You pay a monthly or annual premium creating a bucket of money to spend on care. The size of the bucket is based on the daily or monthly draw rate times a number of months. If a policy pays $3,000 per month for 36 months the bucket has $108,000 in it ($3,000 x 36). Adding inflation protection ensures that the policy keeps up with the rising cost of care. Couples can benefit from a shared policy where either or both spouses can tap the bucket, increasing the odds that benefits will be used. What's the downside to long-term care insurance? Most policies are use it or lose it. Like auto insurance, if you never tap the benefits, the money you've paid in premiums isn't refunded. In addition, long-term care insurance policies have medical underwriting, which means you buy the policy with your health and pay for it with your wallet. This is not a good option for folks with medical conditions. With most long-term care policies, after as little as six months on a claim, you're spending the insurance company's money. I call that **extra money**.

A second option to pay for long-term care is a product that multiplies the asset value of what you pay in. For example, pay $100,000 and a company matches it with an additional $150,000 to be spent on care. If you go on claim, your money is spent first, but if you die and never go on claim, what you paid is refunded to your heirs. Multiplying the value of your money to pay for expensive long-term care is like getting **extra money**. Also, since asset multiplying products usually have lighter underwriting, more people can qualify.

A third way to pay for long-term care is tapping the death benefit of a life insurance policy before death. Many life policies offer riders that allow you to tap a certain percentage of the death benefit monthly to pay for care. Like asset multiplying products, if you don't use this benefit, more money goes to your heirs.

Our final solution involves doubling a lifetime pension. We've discussed the power of having more guaranteed income in retirement. Many of the lifetime pensions we help clients create will double the amount paid for up to five years if our clients need long-term care. Usually the pensions we create have no underwriting, i.e., anyone can qualify.

Commercial products that pay for long-term care can be confusing. My recommendation is to find someone who understands and can explain the pros and cons of each alternative. Or, just give us a call.

Pay Less Income Tax

Every dollar you don't have to pay Uncle Sam is a dollar you get to keep. Think of it as **extra money**. This chapter could be an entire book. That's how many creative tax strategies we've learned over the years. But in the interest of time and printed space, here are some basics. Tara and I do tax planning, not tax preparation, and there's a big difference. Has your CPA explained how our tax system works? Maybe not because their primary job is to help you report and file your taxes, not necessarily to be a tax advisor. We help clients implement legal strategies to reduce the income tax they owe.

Know Your Optimal Gross Income

Our tax discussions always start with a simple question, "What is your optimal gross income?" This is an important question because it identifies which strategies we can use to save on taxes. But first, the basics. Our annual income tax is based on a table where different amounts of income are taxed at different rates. It's called a progressive tax system, because the more income you make, the higher the tax rate. On December 22, 2017, President Donald Trump signed the Tax Cuts and Jobs Act (TCJA) that lowers the tax rates for many Americans. The rates for individuals are scheduled to expire at the end of 2025 (reverting back to the pre-Trump tax rates), so there might be some opportunities in the next 5 years to do some creative tax planning.

The 2017 tax law also increased the standard deduction, the deduction anyone can use to reduce their gross income. In 2020, the standard deduction for singles is $12,400 and for married people it's $24,800. If you are single and 65+ you can add an additional $1,650. If you are married and you and/or your spouse are 65+ you can each add on another $1,300. In the past many

Americans itemized, i.e., claimed individual deductions like mortgage interest and medical expenses, but the new higher standard deduction is what most people claim today.

Refer to Figure 7 to see the various income bands for single and married people. You will notice that single people have a tax rate of 10% on the first $9,875 they earn while for married couples it's the first $19,750. The first two tax bands are 10% and 12%, which are very low rates. If a married couple has taxable income above $80,250, the rate jumps to 22%, which is a lot higher than 12%.

Now to figure your optimal gross income, we add the income limit for the 12% income band to the standard deduction. If you're married that's $80,250 plus $24,800 and an additional $2,600 if you are both 65+, totaling $107,650. If you are single and 65+ your optimal gross income is $54,175. So, where is the **extra money** opportunity? It depends on whether you are above or below the optimal income limit.

Gradual Roth Conversions

If you are below the optimal income level, there's an opportunity to gradually convert some of your taxable IRA dollars to after-tax Roth IRA dollars at the very low 12% tax rate. This opportunity applies to people under and over age 72. In both cases you are converting taxable dollars to after tax dollars. There are no Required Minimum Distributions (RMDs) on Roth IRAs, so as the original owner, you can invest these funds and let them grow tax free. When your kids inherit retirement funds, which type do you think they would prefer, taxable or tax free?

Tax Deferral

What if you are above your optimal gross income? Let's see if we can find some more **extra money**. Let's start by identifying what is creating the income. There are income sources you can control

Optimal Gross Income 2020 Tax Brackets		
Tax Rate	Single	Married
10%	$9,875	$19,750
12%	$40,125	$80,250
22%	$85,525	$171,050
24%	$163,300	$326,600
32%	$207,350	$414,700
35%	$518,400	$622,050
37%	$518,400+	$622,050+
Standard Deduction	$12,400	$24,800
65+Additional Deduction	$1,650	$2,600
Maximum 12% Income	$40,125	$80,250
Optimal Gross Income	$54,175	$107,650

Figure 7

and some that you can't. We can't do anything about Social Security income and pension income. But what if the income that is putting you above the optimal gross income is 1099 income. Are you getting interest income from you CD or bank accounts? How about 1099 income from an after-tax brokerage account? This is income where you have a choice. What if you move your CD or brokerage funds into something that grows tax deferred? Two important things happen. Funds that grow tax deferred grow faster. Why? Because the money you would have paid Uncle Sam stays in the account. Next year's earnings compound and grow faster on this larger amount. **Albert Einstein** famously said that **compound interest** is the most powerful force in the universe. He called it the 8th wonder of the world. The second important feature of tax deferral is YOU get to control **when** taxes are paid, not your banker, broker or some politician. You only pay taxes when you withdraw earnings.

Where do we find products that grow tax deferred, that safely outperform the stock market and that are protected from creditors and lawsuits? You already know the answer. Tax deferred annuities. Maybe they're not as bad as you thought.

This chapter is a tiny tip of the "pay less tax" iceberg. If you have been fortunate enough to build up a sizable IRA, or a highly appreciated after-tax brokerage account, or have highly appreciated property, I have some good news. One of our trusted partners, the Foundation for Financial Education (F3E), is a non-profit, and they specialize in helping our higher net worth clients save big on taxes. We're talking about legal ways to save tens of thousands of dollars that would have otherwise gone to Uncle Sam. That's a lot of **extra money**. The tax expertise offered by F3E is free. Call us to see how much you can save.

Under 60

Most of this book is for geezers (like me). If you're younger than 60 (or your kids are), this chapter is for you. If the goal for retirement is to have more money, ideally tax free extra money, let's define the perfect investment to fund your retirement.

You want the flexibility to contribute more funds, without government-imposed limits based on your income (think Roth IRAs). You want the funds to grow tax deferred. The funds need to increase nicely when the stock market is up, say 10% per year, but never decline when the market drops. Importantly, you want to be able to withdraw what you paid in and all the growth, TAX FREE. You don't want any government-imposed rules forcing you to take Required Distributions (think IRAs). And when you die, you want whatever is left to go TAX FREE to your children. How does that sound? Too good to be true? I think I'm safe to say that most of us would like more **tax free extra money** in retirement that the government can't control.

When I tell you the funding vehicle that does all of the above and more, your reaction might be "I don't believe it." That's what I thought until I learned as Paul Harvey used to say, "the rest of the story." The product is life insurance, but that's NOT why you buy it. I hate life insurance, but I love tax free growth, tax free withdrawals and giving my children **tax free extra money**. Think of life insurance as the wrapper around a bundle of tax-free features. Yes, you (actually your spouse and/or kids) get a death benefit if you meet your maker sooner than later, but that's not why or how you use the policy. Life insurance policies allow you to contribute excess cash. The cash grows tax free, increases in an up market, avoids down markets and is available when you need it TAX FREE.

Today, most folks are pouring money into their IRA or 401k. That's great on the front end, when we get a tax deduction for the contribution. But what happens on the back end? Who knows what politicians will do with tax rates in the future? In December 2019, President Trump signed the SECURE Act. It didn't get much press coverage because of the impeachment inquiry, but it had a profound impact on IRAs your kids inherit. The SECURE Act forces your kids to withdraw all inherited IRA funds within 10 years of your death. If your kids are in their peak earning years, the IRA distributions may push them into a higher tax bracket, and make Uncle Sam one of your biggest heirs. With a skyrocketing national debt, do you think tax rates just might have to go up to service interest payments on U.S. government debt? How much of your IRA do you (or your heirs) want to give to Uncle Sam?

Life insurance, like Roth IRAs, is one of the only products that provides **tax free growth and tax free withdrawals**. Unlike Roth IRAs, funding limits are a lot more flexible. If you are in your 40's or 50's (or your kids are that age) we need to have a chat. Find out how much **tax free extra money** you (or they) can create.

Legal Events Can be Expensive

I am often asked "Are you a lawyer?" My response never varies, "I am not one of that brood of vipers." OK, probably need to soften that a bit. Actually, Tara and I work closely with a number of elder law attorneys. I have great respect for how they help people protect their wishes from life's surprises. This chapter talks about some of the legal things we've learned working with thousands of clients. Since Tara and I are NOT attorneys, we ask that you always refer legal questions to a legal professional. What's included here are my opinions as a fellow citizen.

Protect Your Wishes

What do legal documents do? They protect our wishes. To me, legal documents can be divided into two groups: documents we all need and those that are needed for specific situations such as buying a home or qualifying for Medicaid long-term care benefits. Since the subject of legal documents could easily morph into a multi-volume treatise, I just want to talk about legal documents we all should have. Said another way, if you don't have these documents, you may encounter some costly situations. Avoiding these costs is like getting to keep **extra money**. The legal documents we should all have can be further divided into documents we need while we're living and documents we need after death. The documents Tara and I have found most useful while we're alive include *Financial and Medical Powers of Attorney*. The after-death documents include *Beneficiary Designations*, *Wills* and *Trusts*. Once again, this is NOT a comprehensive list of the documents you may need. There are many other legal documents to consider. Find and engage an Elder law Attorney to pinpoint what you need.

Let's Avoid Guardianship

Many people worry about what happens <u>after</u> they die. Tara and I worry about what happens <u>before</u> you die, if you can't make financial or medical decisions. So, what is a *Power of Attorney* (POA)? It's a document that appoints people to make financial or medical decisions for you when you can't make your own decisions. Why are POAs important? Two of the risks while living longer are accidents and cognitive impairment. What if you have an accident that limits your ability to make and communicate decisions? What if you suffer from dementia or Alzheimer's? Unfortunately, because of these two issues, many people lose the capacity to make their own decisions. And if you haven't taken the time to complete a POA and appoint one or more agents in succession to make decisions, the alternative can be very expensive. It's called Guardianship. Under Guardianship, a judge appoints someone to make decisions for you. And it may or may not be the person you would have selected. Guardianship is a court process and there are lots of costs you may incur. Think court costs, attorney fees, fees to prepare financial records, ad litem fees (court appointed people who represent you), more fees if the guardianship is contested and recurring annual costs. Guardianship is the equivalent of losing a lot of **extra money**. Whoever is appointed as your guardian of your estate has to go back to court annually to explain how your money is being spent. And judges that don't know your wishes control how your money is spent. Here's another example of what can happen: If you are married and jointly own a home, and one of you gets banged up in a car accident, can the other spouse sell the home if it makes sense to downsize or relocate? Without a POA they may have to see a Probate judge for Guardianship. It's important to take a few minutes to complete financial and medical POAs in order to avoid this nightmare. We urge you to get this one done. You never know when incapacity will rear its ugly head.

Let's Avoid Probate

What is Probate? In layman's terms, it's the re-titling of assets after we die through a courtroom process. Here's an example: If you own a house and want to sell it, you have to sign off as the seller when you close the sale. But what if you're not alive? Who signs the document in your place? A probate judge will appoint an executor or administrator for your estate and issue letters of authority that allow the appointed person to sign for you. So, what are the problems associated with going through probate? Probate is not difficult in Texas where Tara and I work. But, over the past several years, we've noticed that some counties now require your executor to retain an attorney for court efficiency. By hiring an attorney your kids will probably spend $2,000 to $3,000 in attorney and court fees. That's a lot of lost **extra money**. Another issue: Probate is a matter of public record. People can see what you give and to whom. I prefer privacy. So, what are the alternative ways to pass assets?

I'm personally familiar with three ways to pass assets after death: using a *Will* (going through Probate), using a *Trust,* or using beneficiary designations. To me, the simplest, fastest and least expensive way is using beneficiary designations. This is what Tara and I recommend to our clients. Putting a beneficiary designation on each of your assets means the ownership changes as soon as your heirs provide a death certificate to the asset custodian. In Texas we can add a beneficiary designation on our homes using a Lady Bird Deed or Transfer upon Death Deed. The Texas Department of Motor Vehicles has a Beneficiary Title naming a beneficiary for your vehicles. And all financial institutions (including insurance companies) allow you to name one or more beneficiaries on your financial accounts. If everything you own has a beneficiary designation, there are no *Will* disputes and no Probate. If you want to use beneficiary designations to pass your assets, it is important to review them on a regular basis.

After all, as time passes, the person you named earlier may not still be the ideal choice.

A final word of caution. Tara and I have seen situations where people try to avoid Probate by adding a son or daughter's name on an asset as a co-owner. This approach does avoid Probate, but it can create some very bad, unintended consequences. If you have a home, the homestead exemption (in Texas) protects it from creditors and lawsuits. Your home is your castle and you can't lose it. But what if you add your son on as a co-owner? Since he doesn't have the homestead exemption, you have just exposed the value of your home to his creditors and lawsuits. Several years ago, a lady came to see me and wanted my help to recover money taken from her checking account. She told me she had added her daughter on as co-owner to make it easier to manage the funds. The daughter went through a divorce and her ex-son-in-law's parting gift was naming his mother-in-law's checking account as community property. Half of her money walked out of the bank, and I had no way to get it back. If you want to add a son or daughter on your checking account, a better way is to add them as a signer NOT a co-owner, and also as a beneficiary. This approach avoids probate and your children's creditors and lawsuits.

Remember, it's up to you to have the right legal documents. Take the time to find an elder law attorney you like and get your wishes protected. Don't procrastinate, do it now.

Walking

It's not how long you live; it's how long you live **well**. Most of us are going to live longer than our ancestors. So, how much of this extra time will we really enjoy? The answer depends on our health, and the maxim "use it or lose it" is apropos. If we keep moving, keep our weight down and blood pressure under control, the quality of life can be much better. Best of all, there's a simple, free activity most of us can do to help ensure our health and reduce future medical and long-term care expenses… Walk.

Walking has been around since the beginning of mankind. Our great, great ancestors stayed in shape trying to outrun wild animals. But in today's technically advanced, automobile enhanced, high-stress lifestyle, walking is seen as, well maybe barbaric? I want to build the case for walking.

You don't need a gym membership, a stationary bike or an expensive elliptical machine to stay in shape. Walking only requires two things: a pair of comfortable shoes and the determination to head out the door and take the first step.

I have been a jogger most of my life. My knees and heels can attest to the pounding they've incurred. My inspiration to start walking came from my business partner, Tara Kendrick. She founded a women's hiking club in Austin. Today, they have lots of members, their own fancy shirts and a monthly schedule to get out and enjoy nature.

My final argument for walking is the National Parks. One of the greatest gifts we can all share is the incredible beauty of our National Parks. My son Jesse and I have hiked Big Bend, Rocky Mountain, Glacier, Zion and Yellowstone to name just a few. Each park has its own unique charm, but the common theme is nature's beauty at its finest. So, where's the **extra money**? When I turned 62, I got a Senior Pass from the National Park system. The one-time fee (it was $25 when I got it) gives me (and whoever's in my car) free access into all of the National Parks. My card has gotten a real workout and saved me a bunch of **extra money**. Of course, **always check with your doctor before starting any exercise regime**. Maybe I'll see you on one of the trails.

Find Your Purpose

We're getting near the end (of this book, not your life) and I want to switch gears. Most of what Tara and I do is on the financial side of retirement planning. But, there's another side, the philosophical side. Some people have wonderful, romantic notions about how great retirement is going to be, and that's OK. But there may be a dark side of retirement we need to talk about.

Some of us identify our purpose in life, our reason for being here, through our careers, or our job. There is nothing wrong with going to work and enjoying the opportunity to help others, to solve problems, to have a purpose for existing. But, if our self-worth is predicated solely on our career, what happens when the music stops?

When Tara and I complete a retirement plan for a family, I often ask a question. "After you hang up your spurs, what will be your new purpose? What will be your new passion, your reason for bounding out of bed in the morning?"

If you've never given the question of purpose a thought, now's a great time to think about it. There are lots of good answers: volunteering, taking a course, starting a new hobby, traveling, joining an exercise class, getting dirty in the garden, playing with the grandkids, continuing to work part time, starting a business, starting a new non-stress job, serving as a mentor, writing a book (like this one), or maybe just keep on working (like me) if you're blessed to love what you do.

Retirement is supposed to be the Golden Years. The time we get to play again, to enjoy life, to share it with our families and friends, to reminisce. Retirement can be great, but not without purpose. If you are nearing retirement, consider shifting to part time to test the waters.

Tara has a sign over her desk: Find Your Purpose. My prayer for you is that you find yours and retirement is everything you hope it will be.

Filter and Process

This book is a filter. After writing the book I went hiking with my son and daughter in Crested Butte, CO. During the trip my son asked me, who did you write the book for, who is the intended audience? My answer surprised him. I said, I wrote it for me. After reading this book you should understand two things: the breath of our practice (the retirement topics where we provide guidance), and our philosophy of using insurance products to generate income as the foundation for a safe, secure retirement.

You should now be "filtered" into one of three categories:

1. You like our approach to retirement planning and want to use our strategies (maybe as a client) to plan your retirement. We're happy to help you!
2. You like our approach but only need help with one topic, maybe selecting Medicare coverage, maximizing your Social Security, or helping your mom and dad preserve assets and qualify for Medicaid benefits in a nursing home. We're happy to help you too!
3. Our message doesn't resonate. You like riding the stock market roller coaster and would miss the thrill of the ride. That's OK too. Tara and I dance to a different tune. The last thing I want to do is sell someone on our approach. It either feels good or you should seek professional guidance elsewhere.

If you are interested in building a retirement plan, we do it in three easy steps:

1. **Create a Baseline Scenario**. We enter your **happy number** (your budget of monthly expenses), your income

sources and your assets into our retirement software. The model is factored for inflation, calculates your taxes and pinpoints where you will be asset wise in 10, 20 or 30 years.

2. **Compare Alternative Scenarios.** We investigate the impact of: when you claim Social Security, down-sizing your Mc-mansion, creating more guaranteed income, retiring sooner, working longer, getting a part-time job, etc. Now you begin to see the impact of your decisions on your financial future.

3. **Implement Your Plan and Measure Results.** This is the fun part. We help you implement your plan and meet annually to see if we are still on target. Retirement is full of unplanned surprises. Maybe your kids move back home or you or your parents need help with long term care. No problem, we adjust the plan. Small adjustments, especially early in retirement, ensure that you meet and exceed your retirement goals.

Free Help

Some of the **extra money** topics I've discussed are easy to implement and you can do them on your own. That's great if you're a do-it-yourselfer (DIYer) person like me. But some of the more sophisticated **extra money** topics, like maximizing Social Security or getting **extra money** from your retirement accounts generate better results with professional guidance.

Which leads to the next logical question… how much do we charge for our professional guidance? Simple answer, much of what we do is FREE to the families we help. Our primary mission is education. Ensure that people understand their options and make informed choices. Our consultations are always free, as are our workshops and webinars and help selecting Medicare solutions.

If you want our help to build a 30 year retirement plan that pinpoints how to maximize Social Security; create additional income to ensure your lifestyle; get **extra money** from your IRA; pay less income tax; avoid paying for long term care; and avoid probate, we charge a nominal fee. The plan serves as a benchmark to measure your progress over time. We review progress annually and make adjustments.

The other area of our practice where we charge a fee is if we help a family apply and qualify for federal and/or state benefits to pay for long term care. As you can imagine, there's a bunch of hours in doing that.

If you like the **extra money** ideas in this book, I'd love to hear from you (bill@srctexas.com), especially to know how you've benefited. If you know of other **extra money** ideas, I'd love to hear about them too. And after this book makes the New York Times Best Seller list, I will consider a second edition including your suggestions. You can also sign up for our free newsletter and check the schedule of upcoming workshops and webinars at www.srctexas.com.

So, here's my final question… Do you want to create **extra money** to enjoy in retirement? If the answer is yes, call us at (512) 835-0963 or visit our website at www.srctexas.com to schedule a face-to-face or video chat. Stay safe and healthy.

Our Trusted Partners

Tara and I have to know a lot about many retirement related topics in order to help you create **extra money**. But, no matter how much we know, there is always more to know. So, it's not <u>what</u> we know, but <u>who</u> we know that really matters. Here's a partial list of our expert affiliates, our trusted partners, the folks we turn to, to help find answers to your questions.

Advanced Underwriting – If you have an income tax question, these guys always have the answer. They are a free resource through us.

Bemis, Roach and Reed Law Firm – Need help with filing a Social Security or Workman's Comp disability claim? These are the folks we recommend.

The Brokerage – They're the best of the best when it comes to answering Medicare questions.

CreativeOne – How do you pick the right annuity or life insurance product for your unique situation? CreativeOne has the industry knowledge and experience.

The Foundation for Financial Education (F3E) – If you want to legally save big on taxes, F3E delivers, and they are a FREE resource.

Andrew Friedmann, Attorney – Why do we office where we do? Because that's where Andy is. In my opinion, he's one of the best elder law attorneys in Austin, TX.

Horsesmouth – Social Security is a lot more complex than most people think. These guys are the #1 Social Security advisory in the country!

KG Advisors – This is our go-to source for market investment expertise. Some of our clients want some of their money in the market. Let me introduce you to Eric Kendrick, President of KG Advisors (He's also Tara's husband).

The Krause Law Firm – The rules to qualify for Medicaid and VA benefits are always changing. Krause knows the rules! If you or a loved one live outside of Texas and need Medicaid or VA benefits to pay for long-term care, Krause has a nationwide network of experienced advisors (like us).

Select LTC – Maybe you want a long-term care insurance policy but you're not sure you qualify medically. One phone call and Select LTC can provide the answer.

Footnotes

1. April 22, 2019 Study by Finke, Pfau Shows Annuities Improve Retirement Outcomes in Retirement 401k Practice, Your 401k News

2. March 2019 Investment Characteristics of FIAs published by Barclays in QIS Insights, co-authors: Andrew Abramczyk, Shilpa Akella, Robert Shiller, Ph.D. and Tao Wen

3. January 2018 Fixed Indexed Annuities: Consider the Alternative published by Zebra Capital Management L.L.C, author: Roger G. Ibbotson, Ph.D.

4. https://fred.stlouisfed.org/series/GFDGDPA188S Federal Reserve Bank of St. Louis

5. United States Gross Federal Debt to GDP, source: www.tradingeconomics.com U.S. Bureau of Economic Debt

6. www.federalreserve.gov/monetarypolicy/bst_recenttrends.htm

7. 2018 3rd Quarter Federal Reserve Financial Accounts of the United States, Tables L118.c and L117.

About the Author

Bill Witt and his wife Melinda have 5 children. They live near Burnet, TX on Lake Buchanan. Bill received a BSIE degree from Western Michigan University, and an MBA from the University of Notre Dame. Early career stints included IBM and McDonnell Douglas. Later entrepreneurial endeavors involved founding or co-founding four high-tech companies. He co-founded his latest startup, Senior Resource Center, in 2002. Bill and Melinda enjoy boating, gardening, their dogs and cats, feeding hummingbirds and hiking the National Parks.

Made in the USA
Columbia, SC
27 September 2020